SERVANT DRONE

Bruno Neiva
&
Paul Hawkins

NEWTON-LE-WILLOWS

Published in the United Kingdom in 2016
by The Knives Forks And Spoons Press,
122 Birley Street,
Newton-le-Willows,
Merseyside,
WA12 9UN.

ISBN 978-1-909443-80-8

Copyright © Bruno Neiva & Paul Hawkins, 2016.

The right of Bruno Neiva & Paul Hawkins to be identified as the author of this work has been asserted by them in accordance with the Copyrights, Designs and Patents Act of 1988. All rights reserved. No part of this publication may be reproduced, stored in a retrieval system, transmitted in any form or by any means, electronic, photocopying, recording or otherwise, without prior permission of the publisher.

Acknowledgments:

Bruno Neiva would like to thank Paul Hawkins, Alec Newman, Bárbara Mesquita, Sarer Scotthorne, Elizabeth-Jane Burnett, SJ Fowler, Tom Jenks, César Figueiredo, Rui Torres and all poets, artists and editors he's collaborated with.

Paul would like to thank Bruno, his partner-in-crime, poet Sarer Scotthorne and everyone Bruno has thanked. Thanks are also due to the editors of *Queen Mob's Tea House*, *The International Times*, and the *Maintenant Dada Journal 9* where some of these poems have appeared in different form(s). Some poems also appear in an avant garde poetry/collage collection, *Place Waste Dissent* (Influx Press 2015) by Paul Hawkins.

Cover artwork: privados um_1 by Bárbara Mesquita. It was previously published in otoliths, Issue 26, 2012.

SERVANT DRONE

Bruno Neiva & Paul Hawkins

#1 (hawkins)

I disassembled the club's DNA Lounge;
back-in-the-day flyers:
archive sale next week.
Some definition's -
how that plumbing inspector
came out to cover…
where?

Here.

The old bar has strict guidelines
for the dance floor area
the body ratio is dense
and nowadays
this raw structure
has several different
enforcers/promoters.

(^^)

#1 (neiva)

Dance floors
have been animated
by the violence of
hierarchy
since the very first
exuberant pelvis
nod

The massive wallpaper
removal
recently championed by
the authorities
is a direct consequence
of the glut of DJs
on the local scene

Also: former gate crashers
scored high on
Big Money Test

Bruno Neiva & Paul Hawkins

#2 (hawkins)

pop
fame
famous
devoured
spat out of the gun
slave to a rhythm, who are you?

#2 (neiva)

café wives, pastoral
machines
distracting me
buzzing excuse me
gone to second-hand
shops
and back just in time
to sip the cliché
and whisper into my ear
why – you're quite young
but not exactly a clubber
(not my tempo gorgeous,
I'm afraid, not a bit)

#3 (hawkins)

gigs
shift
units
tour riders
yellow m & m's
inflatable ego's punktured

#3 (neiva)

what

about

phallic

centred

nostalgia

driven

rise

and

fall

plots

#4 (hawkins)

post-show in the pistachio-glow
of dumb-fluorescence
or maybe stress on a crystal:
digital facia (albino-lemon)
blinks a payment-request for

    2 beta blockers
    a copper-bottomed mocha
    a saucer of lace applause
    one large handful of sidewalk goth
    chrysanthemums

                        total €49

#4 (neiva)

couldn't escape

gy!be at an old theatre

couldn't escape the fact

gy!be at an old theatre

couldn't escape the fact that

gy!be at an odd theatre

#5 (hawkins)

a river
bark to bark a sawdusty film
the earth tilts timber to groan downstream

cut to

oil-frying old timers
peeling Maris Pipers
cardigans and coats rest on the back of chairs

cut to

wooden forks
tomato sauce
the last bus home

#5 (neiva)

commuting expenses and most notably
synthesized cholesterol have both gone up quite
a bit over   the last quarter but still may be
deductible if certain conditions are satisfied (e.g.
street cred flat rate advance payment)
cut to: a pic of a compact street sweeper
tackling litter

#6 (hawkins)

your drunks ignored my mole
as fuel officer is seen dying
for an andrew bocelli snack

#6 (neiva)

from the bed to the foot of the head
from the foot to the bed of the head
from the head to the foot of the bed
from the bed to the head of the foot
from the head to the bed of the foot
from the foot to the head of the bed
:exercising

#7 (hawkins)

because

of england

i'm packed

to feast on

(love 'em)

half price

deficiencies

vows

                                                supremely free

pro test or

#7 (neiva)

post strata fountain pen commuter at eighteen home town beaten up on stage former sweeper cod sod pleading for red card yet no cream no sugar no country thanks for asking though

#8 (hawkins)

and The Kid goes down
with a smack
of reverse-thrust
>>gravity jelly<<
on the 243
to Hackney

Shop names;

   o. Best Mangal
   f. Cleer Bottles
   a. Viet To Go

#8 (neiva)

1) we've just learned that a bargain's been struck they promised to deliver huge business opportunities to those involved they're giving advice they're having meetings that's all any personal gain whatsoever

2) TAPS TAKE FOREVER TO RUN HOT often a result of a badly designed system or one which has been thoughtlessly extended but not upgraded it has remained buoyant during the economic downturn though

3) people don't even feel like they need to be careful about how open they are about it everyone knows what the deal is there's literally no way you can have one without the other

4) CHERCHEZ LA FEMME

#9 (hawkins)

i heart hackney :: the kid trimmed
the fat from kingsland road we skinned we
keelhauled over sizzle-peel oil drum
we sucked :: the kid shaved
on days sharp and nights and mornings and
middays and dawns and sunsets and flossed
late/in/

i heart hackney :: the kid scooped
neapolitan sundae matching chopped nut
sprinkles wheel trim blackberry keys
leisure trousers :: the kid floats up
the stairs in an out-of-date largactil haze a
chess board short empty canteen dude! black slack/
s/

#9 (neiva)

- I can't pretend that my own interest in the matter has always been quite so elevated • however the mood music has been set • through an intensive weekend of talks and practical workshops you'll learn the all-important craft of knowing both what to share and what to leave out • it may be used in combination with many other aid options but I wouldn't take too many risks thus let's stick to it • step one burn all your manuscripts they're not topping the charts anymore so I've heard • step two avoid Cartesian difficulties insofar as it stems from a certain degree of wealth and leisure • yawn • where are the Turkish cigarettes • step three always weigh up the overall risks and benefits and such • boredom's been given a bad press • the same goes for hiccups • so I strongly recommend you to take it easy • it is also important to bear in mind that our app's going through some minor tweaks but do not attach too much importance to it as it's being worked out as we speak •

#10 (hawkins)

We chew our fucking gums raw, high on nightshift CIA amphetamine & punch co-ordinates, dial-up a drone raid. It's air-con dry and four hours into Thursday. Chemtrail traces a lazy flight across morning's lapis sky (burning charcoal, mint tea, a palm full of figs, flies and sand in the honey, a mother breastfeeding). Eyes closed in the shimmy-shimmer; a grey-blue-grey-white sky. Two hundred and seventy nine minutes of The Simpsons later, (blink white-silver-yellow-silver) all that's left out there is half a dog.

#10 (neiva)

YOU CALL IT PROFESSIONAL FOOTING
I CALL IT DRIVEL-MAKING
YOU CALL IT MONEY FOR OLD ROPE
I CALL IT EMBELISHMENT
YOU CALL IT CONGLOMERATE
I CALL IT CAR PARK
YOU CALL IT OUTCRY
I CALL IT BALD PATCH
YOU CALL IT YOUTH TEAM
I CALL IT ACNE
YOU CALL IT BRAND
I CALL IT BOREDOM
YOU CALL IT MINDSET
I CALL IT SMART DRESSING
YOU CALL IT NATURAL TALENT
I CALL IT ACCIDENT
YOU CALL IT GLOBAL
I CALL IT BLOGAL
YOU CALL IT WORKSHOP
I CALL IT SHOP
YOU CALL IT URBAN PLANNING
I CALL IT PANTRY
YOU CALL IT UPBRINGING
I CALL IT REALPOLITIK
YOU CALL IT RIOT
I CALL IT TOUR
YOU CALL IT SPA
I CALL IT SPAM

#11 (hawkins)

Caught short in Dream Doors,
a noodle-speciality-cum-guarana bar,
she made an excuse for
her lacking liquidity;

something about her boyfriend's
2CV obsession,
the politics
of cash vs plastic
(not being what it used to be)
and agreed with the intern
that damn right
black coffee in bed
was better than Chamomile tea.

In this humidity,
lardy breakfast sweat
soaked through
the armpits of her
Joan Jett t-shirt.
The jukebox played
I Can't Stand The Rain
by Ann Peebles,
as she tried to recall
her PIN.

#11 (neiva)

a: over cuppa leafing through situations vacant
b: rolling eyes, hair dyeing tips, pipe dreaming
c: little we know let alone borrowed ideas at five quid each
a: the valves of the heart put under the microscope are but a foil to the best choric scenes
b: as we speak, the canine affection to the martyrs along the brick floor
c: one has not merely to pay for oneself but to yield a certain profit
d: cinema's equivocal position between art and industry accounts for the relations between author and public
e: you see I once married the Oban girl I did
f: something is wrong with the silence but it often proves pointless trying to assign precise meaning to details
g: he forgot his second pint of brown ale before he was sent on his journey; I brusquely took it, left the field of operations and made my way out
/ / / / / / / / / /

#12 (hawkins)

A) BE THEY RECKLESS
RELEGATION PURGES YOU
INTO THE UN KNOWN
                DIS VIBRANCY

C) FUNDING IS LOST
THE BEST DOCTORS MADE ME
RUN TO THE CITY ZOO
          SPLASHED

F) THE OH-SO-BEAUTIFUL
TILES   BRICK
PANTILE   SLATE
          PERCENTAGES

A= FORM STUDIED
IN THE MONKEY HOUSE
TO BE PICKED OVER
AND PRIMED
FOR THE BRIDGE
IS TWISTING

#12 (neiva)

1. how sad and
   so on been
   and gone and
   so on how sad

2. statement you
   are not am
   I statement
   cuckoo clock in

3. all too
   familiar all
   in all mostly
   the patient

4. prior to would
   soon as long
   as prior to
   admission

5. on strike and
   vinyl or is
   it just self
   sugar grin

#13 (hawkins)

shrike
a shirt
& Brooklyn salt
ice
spine
minted poverty

salmon
catch
water

memory a rose tattoo

#13 (neiva)

tour de booze, low-season
enrolment fee, cloaked
in juvenilia,
handkerchiefly (to say
the least) bearing
miscellaneous
sighs, sugar crumbing
along narrow avenues,
coping with attendance,
quarrelling over the correct
usage of the jaw, not a hint
or an inkling, utterly
drunk on the so-called
LIQUIDS

#14 (hawkins)

past perfumes the corner shop today`s sigh is birdsong breathe in morning deep: fried bacon & petrol, kebab sweat sandwiched on the 149 diluted into the office by 08:08   mapping creases on a pigs ear   he's really not lost forever, or a wasted butcher down maple street the salt rust stain on a derelict van (without portfolio scrapped decommissioned) is beautiful at certain times of the day really? like I give a fuck

#14 (neiva)

tips on drying out soggy running shoes, admission fee devoted to some cause, users expect functionality, ink aficionados, share your achievements, users expect reliability, lower back and buttocks and legs, all very simple, run for a bit, users edit photos, the most committed enthusiasts, ankle, help people sleep better, new
to-dos, users expect flexibility, all fields, extremely addictive, cross the gaps in-between, now it's back to schedule, users issue invoices, it may boil down to little more than personal taste, a question that researchers largely neglected to address, 24 years in the trade, you've crossed the threshold chap, all sorts of reasons but there's the underlying one, a greater need for uniqueness maybe, to run as fast as the day they first tried it, a prominent publication, the only snag is that it can't be produced in large scale

#15 (hawkins)

What did you say that arc sliver hair clip thingy (choker)
with ferocious mirror (coil lip)
stabbed inlay (clip thingy)
felt choker (stolen kissy)
indie style attacher (sharky)
pointy star shaped pelted (ten)
tortoiseshell rip curl (stabbed)
starter for ten (oh please don't tell me, let me guess)
sharky (ferocious mirror)
stock in trade (arc)
coil lip (rip)
stolen kissy framed (starter for ten)
pushover was called?

#15 (neiva)

did you? I also had
a very pleasant time
on the train
back home

got some extraordinary you-know-what

red-tape-high
k-noia-style
bill-ss-ba-rahs-remix
recordscolumnschartstablesnoticespostitsreports
err worth the money err indeed

then I overheard some young clerks ASKING FOR
officers, not impostors

(and their cheeks, so soft,
10/10 undergraduate cherubs in smart raincoats,
served cold with latest blackberry dressing on the
side

#16 (hawkins)

Field Notes

Leonard prefers his coke iced ballasting our free-trade ribs winch in the province's hair red black reclining red

an out-of-town warehouse made of mirrors crammed w/black plastic bags crammed w/ till receipts museum of lies

a Matisse circa '52 What about i) creamy paper saddles ii) towel the feel of fingers iii) fronds looking sad on the wall

like a sick two-stroke the MEP played on his constituents' sense of regional ID to score votes//free Pepto-Bismal for life

#16 (neiva)

according to the latest report
we're facing particularly acute redundancies
(so it seems)
and data-related stress
(so I've heard)
also further issues in the pipeline
red tape, baiting, talks
bit of training, bit of counselling
PLUS
higher cortical functions have become partly supressed
: that leaves us with in-house mikado
(and military ephemera)
whilst contemplating the gaps between
one neuron and the next
(barbiturate zen)

#17 (hawkins)

noodle bar marimba up high-in-the-mix
GET IT ON
a citrussy squeezed falsetto ice-blue symmetrical tang
GET IT ON
of red bull chemikal vape hangs over the bar
GET IT ON
dark wood graffito palimpsest of burnt sienna
GET IT ON
a pair of west coast sunset lips bleed in stereo
GET IT ON
to the blue veins of thrash-metal
    hardcore breaking up for landfill
    marching time w/feedback
GET IT ON the drummer started the gig topless maybe he has the virus
GET IT ON we stand back then lean on the tiger balm volume a noodle order is a crowd-surf of worms & eels chopsticks are de rigeur GET IT ON mobile phones thrip squeak & caw w/Twitter it's exploded
GQ makes Blair Philanthropist Of The Year

#17 (neiva)

YOU'RE A GHOST, cleared of charges, double cigarette, yes vote, no-more-check-this-out, finders keepers, breaking pics, you're us, LA, to the chest, LA, another move towards, anti-fee, send in your headlines, LA, still touring, bikers and waitresses, next Friday, on the cusp of, LA, pricing sanction, gaming grip, transports to a halt, LA, mosquito haze, long Hong, LA, a little row ago, LA, the eyes of the square, a star to the centre, LA, I'm Ian Tech, I carry, I bury, I'm Barry, across the Balkans, particularly wet, (I mean) are there any regulations, LA, the main story here, showers League, LA

#18 (hawkins)

                                                            agitate

my drink

                                                           see four

glassed-towers

                                                           shaped

like bad teeth

                                                          tourniquet

this ex-boxer's

                                                           jawbone

skyline

#18 (neiva)

mostly digital
laid-off
beaten-up
half-finished
not a purist
no not anymore
(and I still can't tell the difference between
Dave and Pearce)

8-track kneecap
utterly foam
89.9p. sort of
soaring low
selling out a bit
& associates
(and I still can't tell the difference between
Wall and Wind)

#19 (hawkins)

hundreds & thousands
of a fab lolly
colour the pavement
also
           glyphs
               numbers
                    dashes
                         soft furry
lines
                     & hashes

utility
franchise
language

a snub-nosed ford transit
coughs through a red light
couriers growl w/blips
of right hand
gunning for position

#19 (neiva)

bridging the gap to style inspiration: it all boils down to stimuli a.k.a. mixed fibres

every natural fibre favours certain personality traits, such as bouncing back to shape after having been crushed; this is a smelly process due to acid dips, sprays and radiation

(
still, while
hung to
dry the
fibres tend
to look
so pale
– alas!
)

#20 (hawkins)

dawn slips frm t's night-berth seagulls argue n d distanC

                                              u rug
                                              you hag

d green lyt on d microwave reads six-ten

                             u gobbing camRA slag
                             u rollicking pubescent X

l12 hide n yr soft hips

                                              u clag
                                            you lush

I-spy Betsy stretching outa cot-sleep

                           u cracky blag-shamans lash
                             u shoddy-god nob-dog

d st light`s flicker trns d bedsit N2 a school-disco bad drm

                           u rock'n'roll suitcase shag

#20 (neiva)

STAGE ONE before high piled books frustration is palpable. There's a need to pull back a bit and examine the magic hand of chance. The findings will surely trigger deep concern within the hierarchy.

STAGE TWO in a season of splendorous kiss-and-tell candid masturbation keeps getting us nearer to Heaven.

STAGE THREE it is harder and more professionally dangerous to do the job properly. This is the lowest point in our careers.

STAGE FOUR voices will surely run from hedge to hedge – but this is perhaps unsurprising.

STAGE FIVE (and all the bunkum that follows from it)

#21 (hawkins)

buRn wildly delicious food miles

buRn gentRi fi cat ion

the pentecostal choir leans

left of speakeR stack

bass haRmony

to mis-pRopoRtioned cRoss

#21 (neiva)

we note from your palm lines that you code
I remember the first time I attended a meeting in London ... later we visited a man in hospital who was coded to the eyeballs (= had been coding day and night) and I don't think he even knew we were there
perhaps you should consider taking up mentally stimulating activities, such as reading, crosswords or bridge
thus, we regret to inform you that currently the only available position is still not in position to be made available
(I'm afraid there's a surplus of transistors these days)

#22 (hawkins)

      what that blank canvas has o
nit by night   f
all?

s t   r   e   t   ching
                         n-a-k-e.d.

#22 (neiva)

and all the while
the minutes hand
comes to a halt

tanned uni blokes
outline
so to speak
styles of delivery

and there's
air
there's air in it
air
something that makes a case for itself
air
plenty of it
air
made out of AIR
until proven the contrary
air
so much air
it hurts to breathe in
sharp
uncommitted
sheer
air

#23 (hawkins)

Dear Beloved

God bless you Mrs. Caro and God bless you dear beloved. I got your detail Mrs Person - get your money today, or work? United Stated Countries avoid crime justice. Click HERE you are interested in carrying out.

Yours,

Christoff Stark

International Office of More Building
United States of Rome

#23 (neiva)

up to a third off
it starts to be absorbed in 5 minutes
yeah my mum says the same thing
you better get used to it
oh there's the guy from human resources
what a waste of public money no

you shouldn't be smoking it's not good for the baby

arsenal what about it

just answer the question in a clear voice

know what the solicitor's here

I'm afraid it's pure speculation inspector

his shining armour such a killjoy
what took him so long
he says he wants his money back

she's bright articulate good-looking
add up further expenses
it's a lot of dough
I'm not a charity

push red button and pull
hey it's for your own safety

he's only looking after a witness he's not
cheating on you

guess who I bumped into in the supermarket today
I don't really give a toss

#24 (hawkins)

Shooting
Location: Airport Lounge (or privately-funded hospital foyer)
Director: Donna Bale
Actor(s); Charlie Uncle, Kid Tango, Nipper (dog)
Editor(s): Sal Barchmann, Roger Lazerbee
Login: TTYl4545@nasr____

Dog's gotta booklet. Scoop salmon from the tin onto side-plated white bread. Masticate. Gums, roof of mouth, teeth pop beads of fish-spine. Clench, ripple throat muscles, squeeze the paste past gel-turnstile of tonsils. Dog's gotta bowl. Passively smoke. The sun shines tuneless blue air. I stopped, listened, repaired the cistern. Dog's gotta boss. The washing machine? It's full of rust. Dog's gotta boundary.

#24 (neiva)

channel four
or
channel five
same
neutrogena fingers

televised animal
life
thank
you for your support

thank
you high-heeled octopus eaters
for those late night clunks along greasy
streets

thank
you mid-price terraced life

thank
you navy blue anorak

now sport:

#25 (hawkins)

co-dependence maybe   <the creasing reason to
dro()p anchor   in this-city>

we   **once**   [tongue]
   i ****   [to]   drilled
  shared   [the]   for
levi`s   [pout]   happiness
  hip   with   **to**
    [of]   [intimacy's]   a
hip   [lips]   corkscrew

#25 (neiva)

DON'T WORRY
ABOUT TAKING
NOTES WE'VE
PUT ALL
THE IMPORTANT
STATISTICS ON
A HANDOUT
FOR YOU

#26 (hawkins)

H. scrapes his head on cirrus
bouncing down Grove Green Road
shiny black trousers
polished with age

w/a kiss of grey

smile hidden

he made speakers that bellowed

the bass

// hurt it up

beating air-molecules with Peter Tosh
& Yellowman

a mono voice shadowboxing
hear their argument:

'motorway heat-sunk into side streets'

neither melting!
neither absorbing!

#26 (neiva)

Yes, actually what you said is absolutely right.
The
Volatility. The
Direction. The
Quarter. The
Bit. The
Day. The
Road. The
Overarm. The
Relief. The
Post. The
Big. The
Inch. The
Bane. The
Under. The
At. The
Bang. The
Bye. The
Soap. The
Stamp.

#27 (hawkins)

I nod & suck on can of Tennents Super
nod & suck
nod & suck

both of 'em have hats on
Old Mick's Russian Mafia in a thick fur
Henry's a Bolisha Beacon Day-Glo orange fizz

#27 (neiva)

In line with that
But also a message to them
It's very simple
And it's very much suggesting
Actually those pictures
Surely no remorse
It could be described as
Not quite the endgame yet

#28 (hawkins)

spot the   wandering
star   roving
working   up and down
tight-lipped   pedestrianised shoppers

big   issue
Big   Issue
big is   sue

begins to   pig issue
blood/orange   eyes
split   however
quarter   moons

#28 (neiva)

quicksand: best-known
specialists were inquired on the
matter

quicksand: you must be losing the plot
do not get swayed by emotions

quicksand: we should have
stayed sober but we didn't:
now this was not as
unimportant a detail as it
might seem

quicksand: you'll be pleased to hear
that according to brand new aiding networks
and sister agencies
we're likely to have a general upward trend
in the upcoming year

quicksand: we've always mixed patterns
up to a certain extent,
but never at extremes

#29 (hawkins)

lank fashion offers
no slit of shade
an invitation to treat?

grin how
Jacques Cousteau
grinned

a shark in a
(offal-drop)
frenzy

#29 (neiva)

for counsellors could
be seen playing in the
distance
indulging on spasmodic shrugs
and compulsive cooking failing
once again as adults (and ultimately
as children)

by the end of the day
their
crossed
fingers
couldn't
help
but
uncross
in
a
pastoral
linger

#30 (hawkins)

slap
happy
digits

stab

fluff
clotted
pocket

slap
happy
digits

stab

fluff
clotted
pocket

#30 (neiva)

*still dreaming of empty car parks and 3rd rate hash,
an outdated raver selling paracetamol as ecstasy to
12-year-olds)*
is that you
oh cornflakes
some nerve

AFTERWARD

"In this exhilarating collaboration of high-speed, high-vis alternating poems between authors Bruno Neiva and Paul Hawkins:
the very first exuberant pelvis meets   a handful of sidewalk goth chrysanthemums
the 243 to Hackney   meets   acid dips, sprays and radiation
exercising   meets   leisure trousers
YOU CALL IT SPA   YOU CALL IT POETRY
I CALL IT SPAM   I CALL IT MEETINGS of materials of loss and finding - these are poems full of London and its emptying; its spill and its thirst; its forced-outs and its bloated ins; its riots and its friendships. These are poems full of alternating cities, countries and communities, making the reading experience like getting on a night bus in Hackney, passing through stops in Spain and Portugal, and waking up in Switzerland. These are poems that abound with official and unofficial languages, homes and hang-outs. And ultimately, these are poems I would like to hang out in - and will - before I find the spot they inhabited shut down overnight to make way for a really high-end spreadsheet."

– Elizabeth-Jane Burnett

ABOUT THE AUTHORS

Bruno Neiva is a Portuguese text artist. You can find more of his at: http://brunoneiva.weebly.com/

Paul Hawkins is a poet and co-runs Hesterglock Press. He's been a musician, squatter, tour manager, freelance journalist, gardener, improviser, collaborator and manager of an Elvis Presley impersonator. He studied the art of sleeping standing up and drinking lying down with nearly disastrous consequences; last count he's moved on average every eleven months but only ever owned one tent. His books are Place Waste Dissent (Influx Press), Claremont Road & Contumacy (both erbacce press). More info http://hesterglock.com/

www.ingramcontent.com/pod-product-compliance
Lightning Source LLC
Chambersburg PA
CBHW051703040426
42446CB00009B/1271